Baby animals in savanna habitats

Bobbie Kalman

Crabtree Publishing Company

www.crabtreebooks.com

The Habitats of Baby Animals

Created by Bobbie Kalman

Dedicated by Dexter and Bonnie Crabtree
for Drew Harvey Bradley
We love you!

Author and Editor-in-Chief
Bobbie Kalman

Editors
Kathy Middleton
Crystal Sikkens

Design
Bobbie Kalman
Katherine Berti
Samantha Crabtree
(cover and logo)

Photo research
Bobbie Kalman

Print and production coordinator
Katherine Berti

Prepress technician
Katherine Berti

Illustrations
Katherine Berti: pages 23, 24

Photographs
Corel: page 6 (kit foxes)
Digital Vision: page 8 (bottom)
iStockphoto: pages 18–19 (background)
Photos.com: front cover, pages 14 (leopards),
    24 (bottom left)
Shutterstock: back cover and all other photographs

Library and Archives Canada Cataloguing in Publication

Kalman, Bobbie, 1947-
    Baby animals in savanna habitats / Bobbie Kalman.

(The habitats of baby animals)
Includes index.
Issued also in electronic format.
ISBN 978-0-7787-7733-5 (bound).--ISBN 978-0-7787-7746-5 (pbk.)

    1. Savanna animals--Infancy--Juvenile literature. 2. Savanna
ecology--Juvenile literature. I. Title. II. Series: Kalman, Bobbie, 1947- .
Habitats of baby animals.

QL115.3.K343 2011   j591.3'909153   C2011-902557-4

Library of Congress Cataloging-in-Publication Data

Kalman, Bobbie.
    Baby animals in savanna habitats / Bobbie Kalman.
        p. cm. -- (The habitats of baby animals)
    Includes index.
    ISBN 978-0-7787-7733-5 (reinforced library binding : alk. paper) --
    ISBN 978-0-7787-7746-5 (pbk. : alk. paper) -- ISBN 978-1-4271-9717-7
(electronic pdf)
    1. Savanna animals--Infancy--Juvenile literature. 2. Savanna animals--
Ecology--Juvenile literature. I. Title.
    QL115.3.K355 2012
    591.7'48--dc22

                                              2011013876

Crabtree Publishing Company
www.crabtreebooks.com   1-800-387-7650

Printed in the USA/012014/CG20131129

Published in Canada
Crabtree Publishing
616 Welland Ave.
St. Catharines, Ontario
L2M 5V6

Published in the United States
Crabtree Publishing
PMB 59051
350 Fifth Avenue, 59th Floor
New York, New York 10118

Published in the United Kingdom
Crabtree Publishing
Maritime House
Basin Road North, Hove
BN41 1WR

Published in Australia
Crabtree Publishing
386 Mt. Alexander Rd.
Ascot Vale (Melbourne)
VIC 3032

What is in this book?

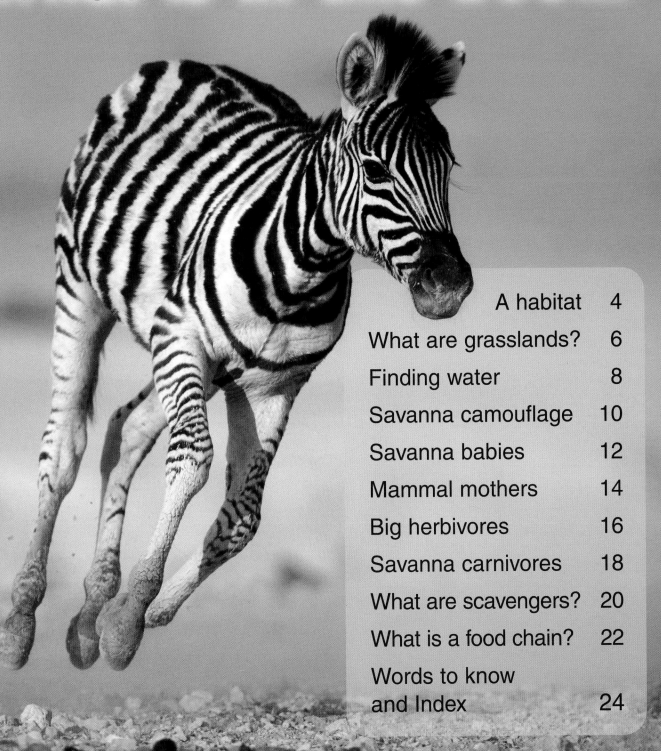

A habitat

A **habitat** is a place in nature. Plants and animals live in habitats. They are **living things**. Living things grow, change, and make new living things. Plants make new plants, and animals make babies. This cheetah mother has six babies. Name two kinds of living things in this picture.

Living and non-living

Habitats are made up of living and **non-living things**. Air, sunlight, rocks, soil, and water are non-living things. Living things need non-living things. They also need other living things, such as plants and animals. Living things find the things they need in their habitats.

Which non-living thing can you see under the cheetahs? Which non-living thing is all around them? Which is shining down on them?

bushes

grasses

soil

5

What are grasslands?

Grasslands are large, flat habitats that are covered mainly with grasses. Some grasslands have a few trees and **shrubs**, or bushes. There are grasslands in many parts of the world. **Prairies** are grasslands in areas that have four **seasons** (spring, summer, autumn, and winter).

This mother kit fox and her babies live in prairie grasslands in western Canada and the United States.

What are savannas?

Savannas are large grasslands in areas where the weather is hot all year. The savannas in this book are in Africa. Savannas have only two seasons—a **wet season** and a **dry season**. Sometimes it does not rain for several months. When it rains, strong winds blow, and there is thunder and lightning. Plants and animals have **adapted**, or changed, to suit the savanna.

These lions are getting wet in the rain.
Which season is it in the savanna?
Give reasons for your answer.

Finding water

Savannas can be very dry places. When there is no rain, plants dry up and do not grow. Animals have trouble finding both food and water. Elephants travel long distances to find water to drink and enough food to eat. They need to eat huge amounts of grasses, bushes, and other plants to keep their big bodies alive.

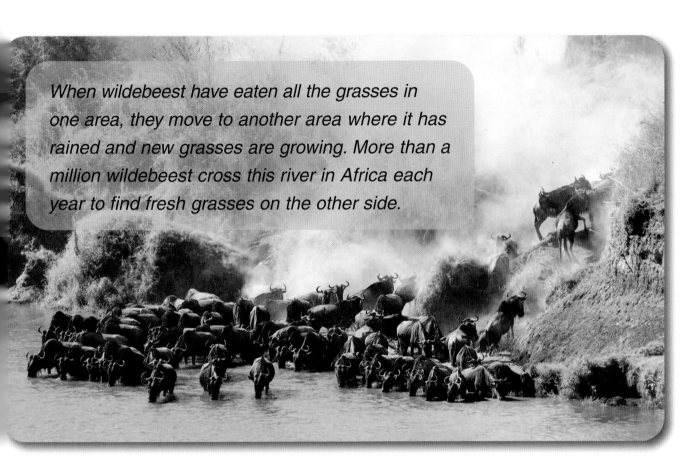

When wildebeest have eaten all the grasses in one area, they move to another area where it has rained and new grasses are growing. More than a million wildebeest cross this river in Africa each year to find fresh grasses on the other side.

This baby baboon enjoys playing in water after it has rained.

9

Savanna camouflage

Many savanna animals are brown with **markings** such as spots or stripes. These colors and markings provide **camouflage** in the savanna grasses, especially in the dry season. Camouflage helps animals blend in with their habitats. It helps **prey** hide from **predators**. Prey are the animals that predators hunt. Camouflage also helps predators. When predators blend in with their habitats, they can sneak up on prey without being seen.

This lion cub is the same color as the grasses around it. Its coloring helps hide it from the prey it hunts.

The brown color and dark stripes on the bodies of these gazelles provide camouflage. They help the gazelles blend in with the dry branches of the trees and bushes so that predators such as lions and cheetahs will not see them.

Savanna babies

These are just a few of the baby animals that live in the savanna. Which have spots? Which one has stripes? Which animals are called pups? Which baby pet animal do you know that is also called a pup? Name four baby animals that are called calves.

leopard cub

zebra foal

lion cub

cheetah cub

rhinoceros calf

hippopotamus calves

African wild
dog pup

giraffe calf

elephant calf

hyena pup

13

Mammal mothers

Mammals are animals with hair or fur. They are born live. After the babies are born, mammal mothers feed them milk from their bodies. Drinking mother's milk is called **nursing**. The leopard cubs below are nursing. Most mammal mothers take care of their babies for a long time and teach them how to hunt or find food.

Baboon mothers carry their babies on their backs while traveling through the savanna grasses.

Hyena mothers keep their babies safe in **dens**, or homes, under the ground.

Big herbivores

Many animals feed on the grasses, shrubs, and trees that grow in savannas. Animals that feed mainly on plants are called **herbivores**. Some of the biggest herbivores on the savanna are elephants, giraffes, rhinoceroses, and hippopotamuses.

Elephants eat leaves, bark, and fruits. They also eat grasses.

Giraffes eat the leaves of tall trees, as well as grasses.

This young hippopotamus is **grazing**, or feeding on grasses, in the evening. During the day, it stays in water to keep cool.

This rhinoceros mother and calf are eating short grasses. They need to eat a lot of food!

17

Savanna carnivores

Carnivores are animals that eat other animals. They eat herbivore Lions, cheetahs, leopards, African wild dogs, and hyenas eat herbivores such as zebras, gazelles, and wildebeest. They also hunt the babies of elephants, giraffes, and other large herbivore

Cheetahs are the fastest land animals. They can outrun their prey. This baby cheetah is practicing running so it can start hunting with its mother.

This leopard has dragged its prey into a tree so other animals will not steal it.

This lion mother has just hunted an animal and is taking her cubs to eat dinner. The cubs are still nursing, but they are also starting to eat some meat. The animal she hunted will feed the whole family, as well as other animals (see pages 20–21).

These African wild dog pups are sharing the prey they hunted.

What are scavengers?

When living things die, they still have energy and **nutrients** in their bodies. Nutrients are the parts of food that keep living things healthy. Predators hunt animals, eat some of the meat, and then leave the rest behind. Other animals get the nutrients from the leftovers. Animals that eat the leftovers of dead animals are called **scavengers**. Some savanna animals are both hunters and scavengers. Hyenas and jackals are hunters as well as scavengers.

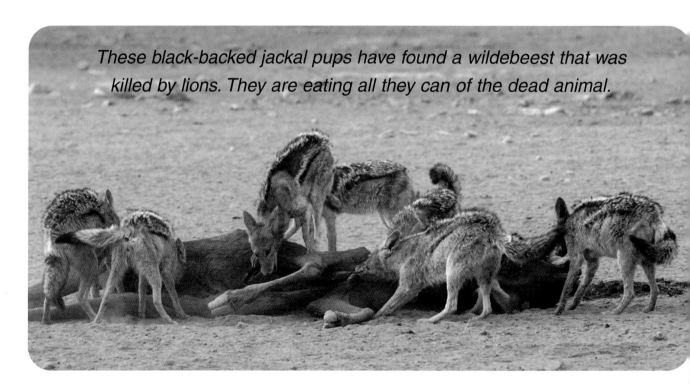

These black-backed jackal pups have found a wildebeest that was killed by lions. They are eating all they can of the dead animal.

vultures

striped
hyena

jackal
pups

This striped hyena will also eat some of the
wildebeest that the jackal pups are eating.
It sees some vultures coming to feed on the
wildebeest, too. Vultures, shown above, can
tear away the thick hides of animals and eat
parts that other animals cannot eat.

What is a food chain?

Animals need **energy**, or power. They need energy to breathe, move, grow, and stay alive. They get their energy from eating other living things. A **food chain** is the passing of energy from one living thing to another. When an animal eats a plant, and another animal eats that animal, there is a food chain.

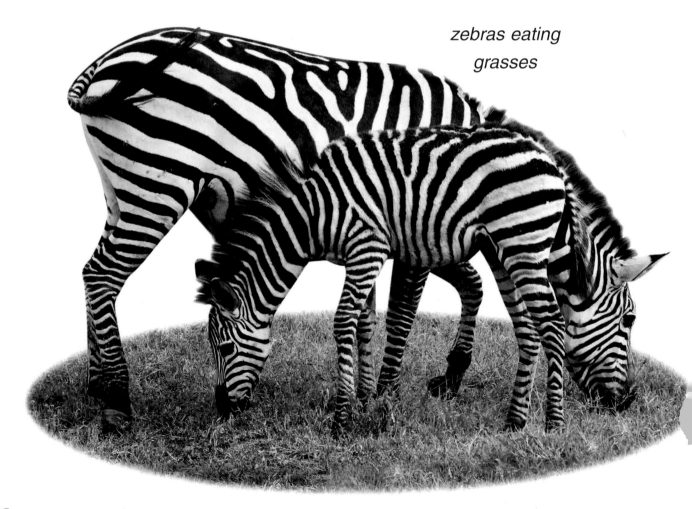

zebras eating grasses

A savanna food chain

This food chain is made up of grasses, a zebra, and a lion.

These grasses have made their own food. They contain some of the sun's energy.

*Plants make their own food from air, water, and sunlight. Making food this way is called **photosynthesis**.*

grasses

When a zebra eats the grasses, it gets some of the sun's energy.

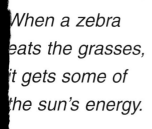

lion

zebra

When a lion eats the zebra, some of the sun's energy is passed along from the grasses to the zebra and then to the lion.

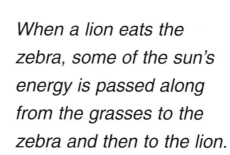

Words to know and Index

babies
pages 4, 6, 9,
12–13, 14–15,
17, 18, 19, 20, 21

camouflage
pages 10–11

carnivores
pages 18–19

food
pages 8, 14,
16–21, 23
food chain
pages 22–23

herbivores
pages 16–17, 18

living things
pages 4, 5, 20, 22
(**non-living things**
page 5)

mothers
pages 4, 6, 14–15,
17, 18, 19

scavengers
pages 20–21